SECRETS

GRA

THE DARK SIDE OF THE WHITE COLLAR

Enjoy!

BY

BELINDA CONNISS

SECRETS TO THE GRAVE

Any reference to historical events, real people, or real places are used through research and where permission has been granted through previous works and or publications.

ISBN: 9798871887080

Printed in the U.K by AMAZON

DEDICATION

Secrets to the grave is dedicated to all who suffered historical abuse whether mentally, sexually, emotionally, or physically in Mother & Baby Homes, Orphanages, Magdalene Laundries, Indian Residential Schools or other at the hands of the Church and State.

It is also dedicated to the thousands of boys and girls not only in Ireland, Scotland and Canada, but around the world who for one reason or another didn't make it.

We must remember them, and the suffering they may have endured prior to their deaths. *(May they rest in peace)*.

CONTENTS

FOREWORD

I had the absolute pleasure of meeting Belinda back in 2017 when she first attended the Sean Ross Abbey commemorations in Tipperary.

Belinda, on that first visit felt in her heart that she was meant to show her support to the survivors and do all that she could to be part of future commemorative events.

In 2017 Belinda had written the poem 'Voices' in dedication to those who passed away and were buried on the grounds, she then went on to write her book. 'Behind Closed Doors' which I had the pleasure of presenting a copy to our Minister for Children Roderic O'Gorman.

I will always remain grateful to Belinda for her show of support and continued attendance coming from Scotland with her husband Jerry both of whom I now consider to be close friends.

Teresa Collins,
Tipperary.

PREFACE

As an advocate and supporter of the survivors of religiously run institutions I wanted to write this book to highlight the atrocities that took place historically with a view to educating those who either aren't aware of such or those who are and wish to know the facts.

Through my research and talking to survivors of such Institutions I couldn't help my own heartbreak and feeling the pain and heartbreak of all connected in some way or another to such a dark time in history.

This book has not been written just to educate but to keep in mind that in todays society we still hear of abuse within religious organisations and it needs to stop.

Unfortunately survivors and or other are still fighting for justice, they/we need the perpetrators not only of historical abuse but that in which is still going on today to be punished accordingly and appropriately.

It is public knowledge that some *(Because not all who wear a white collar are abusers)* who do the work of God, for whatever reason go unpunished and are moved to other dioceses in order to make it go away.

Well, survivors and victims have a voice, their voices must be heard, and the church and state need to listen. They will no longer be kept quiet because as long as they are, then those who commit such crimes will continue to cause long term damage which will, and has affected future generations.

We also want the church and state to take full responsibility by acknowledging that those crimes were indeed committed and to release funding for the work that must be done to rectify those injustices.

The Church who made vast amounts of money through their crimes must pay for the excavations and re-burial and or the recognition of those who died, this must be done in order to bring peace to the surviving families of those who lost their lives. (*Many of whom were very much untimely and unnecessary deaths*).

The Vatican must no longer move Priests to other diocese whereby they can continue to abuse others, they must be seen to strip those who commit such crimes of their ordination.

INTRODUCTION

So many children died while in internment and death camps falsely called 'Indian Residential Schools', those who have fought against impossible odds to recover the memory of those children and the truth of how they died.

Bringing justice to those responsible for those who continue to suffer and die today at the hands of those in the same or similar criminal system, including, those who were incarcerated in most other religiously run institutions.

I am educating you the reader while highlighting just how wicked, evil, criminal and corrupt religion can be.

Sure, my faith 'In God' is very important to me, after all I wouldn't be here without him, but religion on a whole means nothing but pain, sorrow, darkness and in some cases the root to all evil.

What you will read in the following pages is a definitive account of the genocide ever published in Canada *(In part)* including true accounts of the darkness that surrounds other institutions in various other countries and some of those which was told to me during my research.

A genuine, non-government inquiry has been operating in Canada since February 1998.

The Truth Commission into genocide in Canada (TCGC) and its subsequent offshoots. As a grassroots, self supporting network of native and non-native people, the movement has struggled against enormous odds to document and make public the true and uncensored story of the genocide massacre known as Indian Residential School System.

The TRC was deliberately established by church and state in response to the TCGC's independent inquiry and public protests in order to sabotage and defuse the tremendous impact the movement has had since the spring of 1998.

It is up to people like you and me to not only be aware of what exactly is and was going on under our noses but to support those who fight for justice in resolving past atrocities and that of which is going on today.

We must shed light on the legions of missing children so as to give countless survivors their voices.

People must understand that stories like these are composed for future generation of people not only in Canada but around the world to step away from the crimes of the past and that they must not in the future live, fund or collude with those responsible for such crimes.

We live in hope that one day to repudiate that system so they can build a new and just federation of equal nations, and equality for everyone going forth.

Religious Institutions, and others who were also involved in such crimes must understand the pain and suffering they have caused, they must also hold their hands up and admit to that pain and suffering.

We must use our voices to stop history repeating itself and to see those who commit such crimes going forth are punished accordingly.

MURDER BY DECREE

A statement given by Ernie White, residential school survivor, 2011

"I saw lots of free food and fancy suits and rock bands at the Winnipeg TRC, but they didn't have the money to pay our way down from our reserve to tell our story. What's worse, when we tried to get up at the mic and tell about the kids we buried at the residential school we were told we couldn't and the mic was turned off. That (TRC Chair) Xxxx even laughed in our face, and he said, "Oh no, it's those loonies from sandy bay again!"

Canada's Truth & Reconciliation Commission (TRC) Was a rapid in-house response by the church and state designed to present their own self-serving narrative of their Indian residential schools crimes.

It was by any objective standard an elaborate misrepresentation of a monumental crime.

For one thing, the TRC was created by the same institutions and of the church and state that were responsible for the residential school crimes being investigated.

That fact alone disqualifies the TRC from the outset as any neutral or credible body.

Indeed, the TRC only commenced its work after both institutions had legally indemnified themselves from any liability for those crimes, a manoeuvre that constituted an obstruction of justice under the law.

The government's formal announcement of the TRC in June 2008 was triggered prematurely by a series of widely reported church occupations led by residential school survivors in 2008, followed quickly by a call from a member of Parliament for an inquiry of missing residential school children.

These events forced the government to announce the TRC as part of a general residential schools "Apology" issued by the then Prime Minister on June 11, 2008.

The protests and Parliamentary exposure concerning the missing residential school children that prompted this premature announcement of the TRC had embarrassed the government and caused the churches responsible for much of the crime to panic, and insist on exerting oversight of the TRC.

This in turn caused the TRC to operate in a blatantly controlled and partisan manner from its inception.

The Catholic, Anglican and United churches actually nominated all three of the TRC commissioners, who were in turn approved by the government's Privy Council in Ottawa.

Ironically but not surprisingly, this tag team action by the perpetrators represented the same kind of power sharing arrangement that characterised the Indian residential school system.

Similarly, the church and government lawyers who constructed the TRC mandate formed it as a legally toothless body who's findings could not be used to judge or convict any person or group and who's records were censored and exclude any evidence of criminal acts or death in the residential schools.

The mandate even declared that the TRC "Shall not hold formal hearings, nor act as a public enquiry, and shall not name any names in their event" So, since the TRC denied that it was an inquiry, then was was it?

In the words of a visiting South African scholar who observed three separate TRC public events during 2011 and 2012.

"It was all an enormous pretence with very little substance to it. It's a so-called 'Public forum' Were controlled events featuring stage-managed speakers, and were structured to prevent any damaging testimony from surfacing.

Never once was it heard that a Childs death or torture even mentioned. It was remarkable how easily the government pulled off what was such an obvious whitewash".

To compare it to South Africa TRC is laughable.

(*Dr Neil Kruger, from an interview on April 12, 2013 with Kevin Annett*).

No residential school survivor was allowed to speak at such an event unless his or her statement was first examined and vetted by the church and state-appointed "Commissioners", The statement was then stripped of any reference to a crime, a killing or the name of a perpetrator.

The survivor only had ten minutes to speak, whereas no such time limit was placed on officials from the church that committed the crime, who were regularly allowed to use the TRC events to publicly justify and minimise the atrocities in the schools.

Shawna Green is a Cree second generation survivor who tried to speak at the TRC forum in Victoria, British Columbia during 2011, and was prevented from doing so. (Her experience is described at:

https://www.youtube.com/watch?v=5xb1u4S_tbs

As she recalls…

"I was disgusted by what we were put through, I was barred from speaking, straight off, and when I challenged this I was threatened with physical expulsion from the hall.

There were only a dozen or so survivors at the forum the day I was there, and they all looked miserable.

They weren't honoured or given any help or counselling or recognition at all, and they could only speak at the mic for a few minutes".

Some fat act Catholic Bishop was given half an hour to spout disgusting crap about how they were only trying to do good in the schools.

At that point, an old lady who had gone to Kuper Island (Residential School) started yelling out at the white church guy, *"Stop lying! Tell the truth!"* And the TRC Chairman xxxx stood up and yelled at her to be quiet and show respect to the Bishop!

Show respect to your rapist! And Xxxx is supposed to be a native. The old lady looked totally crushed, she looked like something had just been killed in her.

It was like watching her getting abused all over again, such re-traumatising behaviour by the TRC officials was hardly accidental, considering their mandated aim to block unregulated statements, censor evidence and shield church and state from legally damaging revelations.

Police were often conspicuously present at the TRC events, and according to one officer at the Ottawa forum, were instructed to be on the alert for and detain 'Unauthorised speakers or protesters.'

Such intimidation, and the clearly unlawful mandate of the TRC to deny citizens their constitutional right to speak, name their abusers and have their evidence recorded for legal purposes, actually compelled the first head Commissioner of the TRC, judge Xxxx to resign from his appointment just a few months after the TRC was launched.

(See "Chairman quits troubled residential school commission", CBC News, October 20, 2008).

Citing difference with his two fellow commissioners, Xxxx 'Expressed fear that political and bureaucratic indifference could compromise the panel.' But Xxxx referred later to the questionable practices of TRC officials and implied that his position as a judicial officer was being compromised by his association with the TRC.

Such a startling public implication by a sitting judge that the TRC was operating unlawfully did not sit well with the TRC in its course under leadership of Xxxx, a Cree politician from Manitoba who took over as the TRC chairman from judge Xxxx.

Although denying it was any kind of public inquiry or open forum, Xxxx and the TRC nevertheless began staging public events in the major cities across Canada that were wrongly depicted by them as 'Truth telling' forums at which residential school survivors could freely disclose their stories.

In reality, nothing a survivor said at such an event was recorded in any open, public record but rather was kept in a private archive, and the copyright to the survivors own statement rested with the government.

The clandestine record system especially to any evidence of crimes or the deaths of residential school children shared at TRC events in the spring of 2010, Xxxx stated that the TRC researchers had uncovered proof that mass graves of children existed at "Some" schools, but neither disclosed this evidence nor stated when it would be revealed, if ever.

Later Xxxx remarked that the evidence of death or killings could be kept confidential 'For five or ten more years'.

As of February 2016, neither the TRC or government and churches have disclosed the evidence of children's grave sites, despite the continual reference to burials and killings by eyewitnesses and in documents surfaced by independent inquiries.

Head TRC researcher Xxxx of Trent University was picked for his role because of his long and faithful service as a compliant scholar in several government 'Royal Commissions' into aboriginal people in Canada during the 1900's.

Xxxx performed a similarly dissembling role for the TRC by conducting a tightly edited 'Research' of already censored church documents while never revealing his finding in public.

But even Xxxx was forced to admit on one occasion that his research had revealed that dead residential school children were being routinely buried 'Two or three to a grave' at the Anglican school in Brantford, Ontario. (June 3, 2009).

One of the most blatant aspects of this official cover up of evidence by the TRC was revealed in how it allowed the churches that ran the schools to edit, conceal or destroy incriminating evidence in its own records.

The TRC had no mandated authority to issue subpoenas or compel disclosure of evidence or attendance at its events by the churches.

The latter were given months after the TRC commenced to re-organise their archives and remove incriminatory evidence from them.

Such organised duplicity at the highest levels of power in Canada is not confined to the TRC's obfuscation of past war crimes in Canada, but extends to the government's recent efforts to throw a similar fog and misdirection around the escalating disappearance of aboriginal woman and children.

Through my research and having read 'Murder by Decree' I have discovered that the research has established that the crimes and murders committed against children in the Canadian Indian residential school system between 1889 and 1996 were legally authorised, sanctioned and protected by every level of government, church and police in Canada.

All the evidence indicates that these crimes constituted calculated mass murder under the guise of religion and education, and represented a deliberate campaign of depopulation aimed primarily at western Canadian aboriginal nations and designed to strike at their weakest link, their children.

By every legal and international standard and definition, these crimes amounted to deliberate genocide.

According to my research and reading of 'Murder by Decree' The primary agents responsible for this genocide were the Canadian federal government and the Crown of England, the Vatican and Roman Catholic, Anglican and United churches of Canada.

Horrified, doesn't begin to tell of the heartbreak throughout my research at these findings but to know that the Crown of England has been exposed in these criminal matters shook me even more.

At no point in the 107 year period of the residential schools in operation were these crimes ever halted or punished by authorities responsible for the schools, despite continued protests and reports documenting the crimes and a consistently enormous death rate.

The perpetrators were routinely protected and exonerated by both government and church officials.

Native children began dying in droves the very first year the residential school opened in 1889, at an average death rate of 50% The death rate in those schools was on average over ten times the morality level on the Indian reservation from which the children had come.

After those huge morality rates became public in 1903 the government stopped officially publishing any death records of students.

This enormous morality was the result of a deliberate practice by all the churches that ran the schools of housing healthy children with those sick or dying from tuberculosis and denying them medical treatment or care.

In effect a regime of institutionalised germ warfare. *(Look up the report of Dr Peter Bryce, Medical Officer of the Department of Indian Affairs, 1907-9).*

1840-2016

1840: The Act of Union creates a single nation of the former French and English speaking enclaves of lower and upper Canada.

The act establishes what will become of Canada on an explicitly assimilationist basis dominated by the English and committed to eliminating all distinctive cultures, whether French speaking or Aboriginal.

1850: Indigenous nations in Eastern Canada have been decimated by deliberately introducing diseases to barley ten percent of their pre-contact numbers.

Local Indian schools run by the church of England, like the Mohawk school in Brantford, experienced enormous death rates of over 40%.

Tribes West of the Lake Head remain untouched by this plague, except on the West coast where europeans are beginning to settle.

1857: The Gradual Civilisation Act is passed in the Canadian legislature, legally eradicating all indigenous people who do not enfranchise and surrender their land titles and nationhood.

1859: Roman Catholic missions are established throughout what will become British Columbia under Jesuit direction.

Bishop Paul Durieu Creates a model to exterminate traditional Indian leaders and culture and replace them with church controlled puppet leaders, a model that will serve the basis for the later Indian residential school system.

1862: Major smallpox epidemics are deliberately introduced among Chilcotin and other west coast tribes by the church of England missionaries like John sheepshanks. Over 90% of the Indians inoculated by Sheepshanks and other were to die within weeks, and land speculators like Sheepshanks fellow investors in the Hudson Bay Company will then occupy the land emptied by Indians.

"I'm led to believe that the Rev Xxxxxx edited the diaries and travel accounts of the outspoken Anglican Clergyman Sheepshanks (1834-1912) Who went to British Columbia in 1859 to serve as first rector of the Holy Trinity Church in New Westminster"

I would love to have been a fly on the wall when those diaries were being edited.

1869-70: The first failed uprising of the Mixed-Blood Metis people near Winnipeg prompts the Canadian government to proclaim its sovereignty from sea to sea, and commence the building of the national railway, along with massive European immigration onto Western Indian lands.

1870: The British Crown through the Canadian Parliament establishes a 'Clergy Reserve' system granting huge swaths of stolen indigenous land to any Anglican or Catholic missionary who settles on such land, usually near to the advancing Canadian Pacific railway. (CRP).

1873: The Royal Northwest Mounted Police, forerunner of the RCMP, is established as a para-military force with absolute jurisdiction across Canada.

Its mandate includes forceable removal of all Indians from within fifty miles of the CPR, and incarcerating them on impoverished reservations.

1876: CPR lawyer and Prime Minister John A MacDonald proclaims through order in council the Indian Act, which reduces all Indians and Metis people to the status of non-citizens and legal wards of the state in perpetuity henceforth, no Indian can vote, sue in court, own land or enjoy any civil or legal rights.

1886: Following the crushing of the second Metis rebellion the CPR is completed, linking the West and East coasts.

The same year, all West coast aboriginal ceremonies like the Potlatch are outlawed and hundreds of traditional native leaders are murdered or jailed.

1889: The Indian residential school system is launched along with the Federal Department of Indian Affairs (DIA), which supports the schools in partnership with the Roman Catholic, Anglican, Methodist and Presbyterian churches.

The latter two who formed the United Church of Canada in 1925 in Alberta.

The death rate in such schools exceeded 40% in the very first year they opened compared to a morality of barley 5% on the reservation from which the children are taken.

1891: The first official report that documented massive deaths in the residential schools is issued to the DIA by Dr George Orton, who claimed that the cause is rampant tuberculosis among children that is being encouraged by school staff, Orton's report is ignored by the DIA.

1903: The flood of reports by an enormous death rate in the Western residential schools provokes the DIA to cease publishing, 'Total spectrum' death reports amongst children, meaning that many such deaths will now be officially censored by the government.

1905: Indians in Western Canada has been depopulated to less than 5% of their original number, over 100 residential schools were in operation, two thirds of which were run by Roman Catholics.

1907: DIA medical officer Dr Peter Bryce conducts a tour of all Western residential schools and issues a damning report that claimed *"Conditions are being deliberately created to spread infectious disease"* Bryce documents that an average of 40% to 60% of school children are dying because of a routine practice of housing the sick with the healthy, and denying them all medical treatment.

He also claimed that the staff were deliberately hiding the evidence of the genocidal practice.

Nov **1907:** The Ottawa Citizen and Montreal Gazette newspapers quoted Dr Bryce report under the headline…

'Schools old white plague, startling death rolls revealed' Despite this Dr Bryce is silenced by the DIA Deputy Superintendent Duncan Campbell Scott and his report is ignored.

Nov 1909: After conducting further investigations that confirms the murderous practices by residential school staff, Dr Peter Bryce calls for the churches to be removed from operating the residential schools.

Bryce is then fired from his position by Scott and banned from civil service although in 1920 he was said to publish his account in his book 'A National Crime'.

Nov 1910: Despite Bryce's findings, Duncan C Scott of the DIA institutionalised church control over the schools through a joint with the Catholic and Protestant churches.

This contract provided government funding and 'Protection' for all schools, including the use of RCMP to incarcerate and hunt down Indian children.

In return, the churches have complete day to day control of the schools and hire and fire their principal staff.

1910: Later government records reveal that during the first decade of the 20th century, the net population of Indians in Canada declined by over 20% an unprecedented level 'Not explained by any demographic or environmental factors.'

The use of residential schools as a breeding ground for infectious diseases that is then disseminated through native communities is the one factor in this depopulation.

Feb 1919: Despite the continuing high death rates and murderous conditions in the residential schools, Duncan C Scott abolishes all medical inspection in them and prohibits further studies of health conditions in the schools.

Within a year, the death rates in Western native communities had nearly tripled. This morality is also caused by a routine practice of sending sick children home to their families with smallpox and tuberculosis.

June 1920: Prime Minister Arthur Meighen states in Parliament that no provision for the health of Indians was ever included in the

Federal health Act or Department. 'It was purposely left out of the Act.' *(See figure 7).*

July 1920: Incarnations in the residential schools is made mandatory under federal law passed through the order of council. Every Indian child seven years or older must attend school or their parents will be jailed. *(See figure 8)*

July 1924: A state church is created by an Act of parliament, the United Church of Canada to 'Canadianise and Christianise the foreign born and the heathen.' The foundational genocidal purpose of affirmation not only through the churches operation of residential schools and Indian hospitals where Indian children die en masse, but in their foundational policy statements concerning their aim to 'Dispossess' aboriginals of their traditions.

May 1925: Provisional laws in British Columbia and Alberta, were most unassimilated, Indians are concentrated, strip aboriginal people of the right to consult or hire a lawyer, or even represent themselves in a court of law. Neither is any lawyer allowed to take on an aboriginal client.

1929-1933: Sexual sterilisation laws are passed in both provinces legislatures allowing any inmate of the residential school to be involuntary sterilised at the decision of the schools principal, a church employee, thousands of children and adults are sexually neutered by these laws.

The Canadian government relinquishes its traditional legal guardianship over Indian children and grants such power to the residential school principal, a church employee.

Feb 1934: An attempt by the government to abolish residential schools is thwarted because of pressure and threats by all the churches running the schools.

Oct 1935: A genocidal 'Two standards of health care' system in residential schools is confirmed by Dr C. Pitts in a letter to the states. E;g *'Were I to apply the standards of health to them (Indians) that is applied to the children of white schools, that (sic) I should have to discharge 90% of them and there would be no schools left.'* Pitt is referring to the Lejac Catholic School In Northern British Columbia, and admits that a lower standard of health care is applied to them.

1937-38: School records confirm that children infected with tuberculosis are admitted to the West Coast Indian schools, and officials refer to the fact that the Indian Affairs Department, *'Will not hospitalise Indians suffering from pulmonary tuberculosis.'*

Jan 1939: Cowichan Indian children were widely used in medical experiments conducted by 'German speaking doctors' at the Catholic kuper Island School in British Columbia. Many of them died, according to two survivors, but the RCMP suppressed inquiries by local police.

1940-45: Under the cover of war, involuntary experimental research had commenced on many residential school children by the Defence Research Board (DRB) in Ottawa.

The research included drug testing, deliberate starvation, behaviour modification, pain threshold studies, chemical weapon testing and sterilisation methods.

These tests were conducted in schools, at military bases, and at special laboratories and Indian hospitals run jointly with the United, Anglican and Catholic Churches.

1946-8: Hundreds of Nazi SS doctors and researchers were granted citizenship in Canada under the joint British-American 'Project Paperclip' who worked under cover identities and military supervision in the aforementioned experimental programs.

1958: The government again attempts to close residential schools and meets with hostile resistance and threats of political action by all three churches operating the schools, the plan is dropped.

1960: Revisions to the revised statuses of British Columbia legally define an aboriginal as an 'Uncivilised person', destitute of the knowledge of God and of any fixed and clear belief in religion or in a future state of rewards and punishment.

1962: A government plan later entitled the 'Sixties Scoop' covertly to privatise residential schools by transforming large numbers of Indian children to non-aboriginal homes throughout state-subsidised foster agencies.

Thousands of children had their identity and family life destroyed in this manner without setting foot in a residential school.

1965: Government document destruction teams obliterated countless residential school records relating to the identity and deaths of students, in anticipation of the phasing out of the schools.

1969: Indian Affairs Minister and future Prime Minister Jean Chretien affirms an 'Assimilation' policy of legally exterminating native nations in a federal 'White Paper' Introduction in parliament.

1970: Native protests against White Paper, including the seizure and occupation of Bluequills residential school in Alberta by aboriginal parents, forces the government to begin the process of turning over residential schools to the control of the local tribal councils.

1972: The government destroyed thousands of Indian Affairs records including personal files with information on residential school history and aboriginal land deeds, making the verification of school crimes and native land claims impossible.

1975: A majority of residential schools formerly run by the churches were now either closed or under the management of local Indian band councils. Nevertheless, many of the same crimes and tortures against children continue, often at the hands of the aboriginal staff members.

1982: The government funds and establishes the puppet aboriginal organisations known as 'Assembly of First Nations' (AFN) Consisting of 600 self-appointed state funded tribal 'Chiefs.'

The AFN claims to represent all aboriginals in Canada, but it refuses all calls for indigenous sovereignty or to investigate the residential schools.

Oct 1989: Nora Bernard an East Coast native of the Shubenacadie Catholic residential school, commences the first lawsuit against both the church and the government for harm she suffered, Nora refers to 'Our genocide.' She may have been murdered in the December, 2007 just prior to the launching of the government cover up known as the 'Truth and Reconciliation Commission.' (TRC)

Oct 1990: AFN head and government employee 'Chief' Phil Fontaine, in response to the Nora Bernard residential school lawsuit, speaks publicly of 'Abuses' In the schools and establishes a benign AFN monopoly over the issues that never mentions the death of children or genocide.

Mar 1994: In Port Alberni, the killing of children in the local United Church residential school is addressed by the Rev. Kevin Annett and native survivor from his pulpit. Annett is told by the church officers to refrain from addressing the issue and is threatened with being fired.

Jan 1995: Kevin Annett is fired without cause after reporting more serious stories of the residential school killings and of the theft of west coast native land by his United Church employer and their business partner the logging company MacMillan-Bloedel.

His unusual firing is addressed by a Vancouver Sun Columnist that summer, as MacMillan-Bloedel issues a payoff to the United Church in Port Alberni. *(See figures 18a, 18b)*

Dec 1995: The first account of the murder of a residential school child, Maisie Shaw is made, eyewitness Harriett Nahanee at a rally held by fired Kevin Annett, and is reported by the Vancouver Sun newspaper. *('Murders alleged at residential school' by Stewart Bell, Vancouver Sun, December 13, 1995).*

A week later, a second such murder, of a boy named Albert Gray, is reported by eyewitness Archie Frank, and is again reported by the Sun *('Beaten to death for the theft of a prune' by Mark Hume, Vancouver Sun, December 20, 1995).*

Both witnesses claim the killer was Principal Alfred Caldwell, the RCMP refuses to investigate.

Feb 1996: The first class action lawsuit by residential school survivors in Canada opens in the British Columbia Supreme Court, brought by fifteen former students at the Alberni school against the United Church and government, Kevin Annett is an advisor to the plaintiffs.

Feb 3, 1996: The United Church begins closed, internal disciplinary proceedings against Kevin Annett to permanently expel him from the ministry, which will occur the next year at a cost to the church of over $250,000

Annett will never be charged by the church with any wrongdoing. The church secretly pays Annett's former wife to divorce him and with the conclusion of provincial court judges rob him of his two children. *(See figure 22).*

1997-98 Other Canadian newspapers begin to report eyewitness allegations of killings in residential schools, including those gathered in healing circles convented by Kevin Annett and Harriett Nahanee.

Feb 9, 1998: At a public rally of over 600 people in Vancouver, many of them aboriginal, the Truth Commission into Genocide (TCGC) is established as an independent open inquiry into residential school crimes, Kevin Annett is elected as its General Secretary.

Jun 6, 1998: Justice Donald Brenner of the British Columbia Supreme Court rules that the United Church and government of Canada are equally liable for damages to the inmates in residential schools, opening the door to thousands of subsequent lawsuits by survivors against all three churches.

Jun 12-14, 1998: The first independent inquiry in residential school crimes is uncovered in Vancouver by the United Nations affiliate, IHRAAM, upon the invitation of TCGC leaders Harriett Nahanee and Kevin Annett.

The inquiry hears from twenty-eight eyewitnesses to these crimes and concludes that 'Every act defined adds genocide under international law occurred in Canadian Indian residential schools'

None of the church and government officials subpoenaed by, IHRAAM respond or refute the claims.

IHRAAM recommends to United Nations High Commissioner Xxxx Xxxxxxxx that an international tribunal be held into these crimes, but Xxxxxxxx never replies.

Jun 20, 1998: The Globe and the Mail are the only media in Canada to report the IHRAAM hearings.

Autumn 1998: A public smear and misinformation campaign is mounted for the first time against Kevin Annett and the TCGC. IHRAAM silences the inquiry participants and buries the report.

Oct 27, 1998: The province newspaper reports an admission by the United Church lawyers that the church has engaged in a cover up of residential school crimes with the government since at least 1960, and that church officials kidnapped children to bring them into the school.

Jan 1999: The residential school crimes and the IHRAAM - TCGC inquiry are reported for the first time outside of Canada, in the British magazine, *The New International.* But the publication is pressured by the crown lawyers to desist from any subsequent coverage of the issue. *(See figure 32).*

Mar 1999: In response to the IHRAAM inquiry and escalating lawsuits, the Canadian government creates an 'Aboriginal Healing fund' (AHF) that is used for a hush fund for survivors.

Any of the AHF recipients must first agree to never sue the government or churches that ran the schools. *Go figure!*

Apr 26, 2000: In the first of many 'Spin doctoring' of residential school atrocities, Health Canada admits that it conducted 'Limited' experiments on school children during the 1950s by denying them dental care, food and vitamins, but provides no details.

2000-2001: Facing over 10,000 individual lawsuits by school survivors, the government under church pressure legislates a limit on the scope of such lawsuits and assumes primary financial liability for residential school damages, ignoring the Brenner joint liability legal decision of 1998.

Crown courts in Alberta and Ontario impose similar restrictions and deny survivors the right to sue church and state for genocide.

Feb 1, 2001: The TCGC publishes the first documentation of deliberate genocide in Canadian residential schools. '*Hidden from History: The Canadian Holocaust' by Kevin Annett).*

Over 1000 copies were sent to the media, politicians and many residential school survivors.

Aug 14, 2001: The British Columbian Court of appeals, under government pressure, reserves the 1998 Brenner decision and places the entire financial liability for residential school damages on the federal government and taxpayer, absolving the churches of any financial liability.

2001-2004: The TCGC mounts a broad public educational campaign about the residential schools genocide, picketing the churches responsible and holding public forums across Canada at which survivors tell their stories and name names.

The commission begins its own radio programme on Vancouver Co-Op radio, the programme would run for nine years until it is terminated from government pressure.

Dec 29, 2004: After being contacted by Kevin Annett, a federation of Mayan Indigenous groups issues a 'Denuncia' or official demand to the Canadian government to disclose its evidence of the genocide of native people in Canada.

Receiving no reply, the Mayans take their Denuncia of the Canadian genocide to the United Nations.

Apr 15, 2005: The TCGC and its affiliate The friends and relatives of the disappeared (FRD) Hold the first 'Aboriginal Holocaust Remembrance Day' in Vancouver outside Catholic, Anglican and United churches.

For the first time speakers issue a call for the repatriation of the remains of the children who died at the residential schools, the event was widely reported in the media.

Mar-Oct 2006: Numerous accounts of mass graves of children at or near former residential schools are received by the TCGC and FRD, prompting the production of the first documentary film on genocide in Canada: 'Unrepentant' The film is based on `Kevin Annett's research and work with the survivors. On oct 1, the TCGC merges with FRD into one organisation.

Jan-May 2007: Unrepentant is released worldwide to hundreds of thousands of viewers, and wins best documentary at the Los Angeles Independent Film festival. FRD and Kevin Annett commence high profile occupations of Catholic, Anglican and United Churches in Vancouver, Winnipeg and Toronto, which are widely reported in the media.

A report surfaces that residential school documents were deliberately destroyed by the government.

Apr 2007: After seeing Unrepentant, member of parliament Gary Merasty Mallon on the government to begin repatriating the remains of residential school children, Indian Affairs minister Jim Pence announces a 'Missing Children's Task Force' that never convenes, but Prentice also hints at the formation of a 'Truth and Reconciliation Commission' to investigate residential school deaths.

Apr 24, 2007: Based on interviews with Kevin Annett and his network of survivors, the Globe and Mail newspapers publishes a front page article confirming the 50% death rate in residential schools.

'Natives died in droves as Ottawa ignored warnings' (Globe and Mail April 24, 2007)

Jan-Mar 2008: The government stalls, FRD launches a new wave of church occupations and declares its intent to begin an action in international courts of justice against the Catholic, Anglican and United Churches by aboriginal elders across Canada.

'Native group warns of international court action' (The National Post, Feb 13, 2008; "Show us where dead bodies are buried, natives ask", (Toronto Sun, Feb 5, 2008).

'Protesters storm church in bid to learn fate of aboriginal children' (The Globe and Mail, Mar 10, 2008).

'Native protesters disrupt Easter service in Vancouver', (The Globe and Mail Mar 24 2008)

Apr 10, 2008: Kevin Annett and FRD release to the world media a list of twenty-eight mass grave sites at or near former Indian residential school across Canada. Neither Annett nor any FRD is ever contacted by the police or government about the grave sites.

Apr 15 2008: On the FRD's fourth Aboriginal Holocaust Memorial Day, the government issues a statement that although 'Enormous numbers of deaths' occurred in residential schools, no criminal charges will be laid against the churches that ran the schools, thereby legally indemnifying them from any prosecution.

The churches then all quickly endorsed the proposed 'Truth and Reconciliation Commission'.

Jun 1, 2008: The Truth and Reconciliation Commission (TRC) is launched by the government after it's officers are nominated by the three churches and approved by the Prime Minister's office.

Its restricted mandate forbids it from laying criminal charges, issuing subpoenas, investigating homicides or taking down as evidence the names of any residential school perpetrators, and over half of all school survivors are disqualified from any compensation by the government.

Jun 11, 2008: Prime minister Stephen Harper issues a formal 'Apology' In parliament for Indian residential schools, not mentioning the deaths of students or the involvement of churches in the schools.

But Bloc Québécois leader Gilles Duceppe refers to the mass graves of Indian children.

Jun 15, 2008: FRD calls on all Canadians and school survivors to reject the apology and boycott the TRC and seek instead an international criminal tribunal into Genocide in Canada with the power to subpoena, arrest and prosecute.

Jan 2009: Unrepentant is now viewed worldwide and prompt human rights groups in Europe to invite Kevin Annett and FRD members to speak at public forums in London, Dublin, Paris and Rome.

The government's TRC responds to each new action by the FRD by holding public forums for survivors, but the latter are discouraged from naming names and describing crimes other other than physical and sexual abuse.

Oct 2009: Italian Politicians, including the provincial government of Liguria in Genoa, agree to sponsor an inquiry into Genocide in Canada after an FRD delegation including Kevin Annett presents them with the evidence and wins their endorsement.

Kevin conducts a public exorcism outside the Vatican, next day, a tornado strikes the centre of Rome.

That week, European media first begin to report the personal complicity of Pope Benedict, Joseph Ratzinger, in concealing crimes against children in the Catholic Church.

Dec 14, 2010: FRD organiser and residential school survivor Binger Dawson is beaten to death by three Vancouver policemen, according to eyewitness Ricky Lavallee.

The cause of death is listed as 'Alcohol Poisoning' Although an accompanying toxicology report states that no alcohol or drugs were found in the bloodstream. Bingo is the first of six FRD members who will die of foul play between 2009 and 2012. *(See figure 47,48 including Coroners report).*

Apr 1-4, 2010: Sponsoring Italian Politicians host Kevin Annett and the FRD delegation of residential school survivors at a major press conference in Rome.

Their support is suddenly curtailed and the FRD delegation is detained by the police just before they are to protest outside the Vatican.

A Canadian government-paid operative has infiltrated the FRD and discredited it to media and FGRD supporters with false stories.

Apr 15-16 2010: Kevin Annett holds high profile protests with Irish survivors of Catholic Church torture outside the Irish Parliament in Dublin, and calls for the public prosecution of Pope Benedict.

'Abuse in Canadian residential schools identical to here, says clergyman'. *(The Irish Times, April 16, 2010).*

'Survivors demand truth panel probe claims on care institutions', *(The Irish independent, April 16, 2010).*

Kevin's trip was sponsored by three groups of Irish survivors of church crimes.

Jun 15, 2010: The International Tribunal into Crimes of Church and State (ITCCS) is established in Dublin by six organisations and survivors of church tortures.

Its mandate is to prosecute both church and state for crimes committed against children, and disestablish such unlawful authorities.

The Canadian government's TRC issues a statement the same week that its research has uncovered evidence of the graves of children at residential school sites, but gives no details.

Aug 2010: The film Unrepentant is broadcast in four languages to over ten million on Swiss and German television.

Kevin Annett's book Unrepentant: Disrobing the Emperor Is published in London, but on Aug 9, Kevin's long standing radio programme Hidden from History is cancelled without cause or explanation by Vancouver Co-op radio, which is government founded.

Apr 10, 2011: Ten Mohawk elders invite Kevin Annett to their territory at Brantford, Ontario to assist them recovering the remains of the children in mass graves next to the oldest residential school in Canada, the Mohawk institute, and run by the church of England.

The next month on May 29, while doing archival research in London, Kevin is deported from England without cause.

Oct-Dec 2011: The ITCCS and Mohawk elders begin their joint investigation into the missing children at the Brantford school by employing ground penetrating radar.

Suspected grave sites are located almost immediately based on surviving eyewitness account.

Actual excavation of such a site commences in the November, and uncovers buttons off school uniforms and sixteen bone samples, one of which is confirmed by forensic experts to be from a small child.

The first recovery of bones from a residential school grave goes completely unreported in the Canadian media, despite a Mohawk press conference. *(http://itccs.org/mass-grave-of-children-in-canada-documented-evidence/).*

Jan 2012: The Mohawk evacuation is sabotaged by paid government agents in the local tribal council, but two remaining elders and the ITCCS publish their findings before the world.

The same month, the government's TRC releases its Interim Report that confirms that an unstated number of children died in residential schools without naming the names of who is responsible.

Jul 1, 2012: Encouraged by the Brantford dig findings, the ITCCS convenes the International Common Law Court of justice (ICLCJ) in Brussels.

The court commences a criminal trial that charges Canada and its churches.

The Crown of England and the Vatican with Genocide and crimes against humanity, and encouraging in a criminal conspiracy.

Thirty defendants are names and subpoenaed, including Queen Elizabeth *(Now Deceased)* Pope Benedict (*Now Deceased*) and Prime Minister Stephen Harper, none of them respond to or contest any of the charges or evidence brought against them in the court. (See **http://itccs.org/common-lae-court-document**/*)*

Now no longer available to view online? Why doesn't that surprise me.

Feb 11, 2013: The chief defendant in the ICLCJ trial, Pope Benedict (Joseph Ratzinger) resigns suddenly from his office just five days after the Vatican receives a diplomatic note from the Spanish government announcing that, based on the ICLCJ court material, an arrest warrant against Ratzinger could be issued if he enters Spanish territory.

Feb 25, 2013: The ICLCJ court and jury find Joseph Ratzinger and all of the other defendants guilty as charged of crimes against humanity and engaging in a criminal conspiracy.

Defendants are sentenced in absentia to twenty-five years in prison without parole and a loss of their assets and authority.

Arrest warrants were issued against the guilty on Feb 25. *(See figure 56).*

Apr-Aug 2013: Three other Vatican officials who are named as defendants in the ICLCJ case and eventually found guilty under its verdict will resign from their offices. Tarcisio Bertone, Vatican secretary of State, Irish Cardinal Sean Brady and eventually, Jesuit leader Adolfo Pachon.

Apr-Jul 2014: The ICLCJ convenes a second case to charge three top Vatican officials with aiding and abetting child trafficking and homicide.

Pope Francis (Jorge Bergoglio), Jesuit head Adolfo Pachon, and archbishop of Canterbury Justine Welby.

Based on the testimony of 29 eyewitnesses linking all three defendants to the 9th circle cult, all are found guilty as charged and sentenced in absentia to life imprisonment. Common law arrest warrants were issued.

Jan 15, 2015: Based on the conviction and legal nullification of the authority of the Crown of England resulting from the ICLCJ verdict of Feb 25, 2013 patriots in Canada declare the establishment of a Sovereign Republic of Kantana under the authority of International and Common Law.

Stand down orders are issued to all Crown agents in Canada and a Constitutional Convention is announced.

Jun 3, 2015: Canada acknowledged that Genocide occurred within the Indian residential school system and that thousands of children died as a result. *(New York Times, Jun 3, 2015).*In response, the ICLCJ convenes a new coalition that will establish the International Tribunal for the disappearance of Canada (ITDC) the following December.

Mar 1, 2016: Counter report to the TRC's misinformation is issued by the International Tribunal for the disappearance of Canada (ITDC) and Kevin Annett.

(Copies have been obtained via Kevin Annett and his writing of 'Murder by Decree' The Crimes of Genocide in Canada). I give thanks to Kevin Arnott for allowing his material to be used for my book.

While now we are seeing some changes within the church in how it deals with sexual abuse it doesn't mean that the secret system has been eradicated.

The Vatican's Secret Archives were first collected and stored in some systematic order in Rome's Castel San't Angelo (Hadrian's Tomb), in 1611-1614 they were moved to the Vatican.

We are led to believe that there are many secrets held in the Vatican with sexual abuses being one of its biggest secrets.

The atrocities of the clergy are like water off a ducks back when it comes to the church, lessons have not been learned, because they continue to ignore the one factor in all abuses caused by clergy, that being, the victims mental wellness.

The church doesn't seem to understand or acknowledge the profound impact on the abuse victims or their families.

Instead of holding the perpetrators to account and helping the victims to recover from such horrendous acts of abuse, they ship the abuser off to another diocese.

What they fail to realise (*Or perhaps they do*)? That the abuser is free to carry out such acts in the new diocese leaving that congregation unaware that they have a sexual predator on their watch.

In the eyes of a child, a priest is someone they should trust because they represent God, unfortunately the priest use their position of power and trust to scare children into thinking its what they are meant to do.

The church wonder why the congregation is whittling away, let's be honest, would you send your child to church unaccompanied? I wouldn't because they have lost my and many others trust.

they looked carefully after their interest in fixing the terms of the surrender.

Mr. CAHILL: If the minister will put the terms on the Table to-morrow, that will be satisfactory.

Mr. McKENZIE: In this appropriation there is an item of $10,000 to prevent the spread of tuberculosis. I am sure that throughout Canada a great deal of sympathy is felt for the Indians on account of the ravages that tuberculosis and smallpox are making amongst them. I was going to suggest to the minister that this is a possible opportunity of handing over this branch of the work of the Indian Department to the Health Department, unless that has been done already. I do not know that there is any phase of the work of the Health Department that is more important than that of making proper provision for the health of the poor Indians. I understand that frightful ravages are being made amongst them by tuberculosis, and their conditions of life are certainly not such as to preserve them from the ravages of that deadly disease. I should be pleased to know that at the earliest possible moment that that branch of the department was going to be transferred to the Department of Health and that proper steps would be taken to look after these Indians. I am sure that even though we are striking hard for economy now, if more money is wanted for this purpose the people of this country would be willing to spend it.

Mr. MEIGHEN: The Health Department has no power to take over the matter of the health of Indians. That is not included in the Act establishing that department. It was purposely left out of the Act. I did not think, and I do not think yet, that it would be practicable for the Health Department to do that work, because they would require to duplicate the organization away in the remote regions where Indians reserves are, and there would be established a sort of divided control and authority over the Indians which would produce confusion and insubordination and other ill effects among the Indians themselves. However, we get every possible assistance from the Health Department. The deputy minister advises me that Dr. Amyot, the Deputy Minister of Health, and his officers have been enthusiastic in their co-operation with the Indian Department in connection with the recent ravages and health matters generally.

Mr. McKENZIE: I am not so much concerned, nor are the people of this country, as to which department does this work, as that it be done. I am not speaking for myself but for a great body of Canadian people.

Mr. ROSS: What is the policy of the department in regard to the employment of medical attendants for the several reserves throughout the country? Is the policy the same in every province? If not, what is the policy in regard to this matter in the province of Ontario? Are the medical men who are employed paid fixed salaries? Who appoints them? Upon whose recommendation are they appointed, and what is the policy generally?

Mr. MEIGHEN: They are usually, though not always, paid a fixed salary. It depends upon the circumstances, the amount of work there is to do, and the availability of a man to do it. There may be a man available whom you can get to do the work incidentally, and not a man available whom you can get to do the work on salary. These two factors control. The Civil Service Commission in every case appoints the salaried men.

Mr. ROSS: These medical men?

Mr. MEIGHEN: Yes.

Mr. ROSS: Since how long?

Mr. MEIGHEN: Since the Act came into effect. There is no patronage.

Mr. BUREAU: The second item under the head of "General" is "relief to destitute Indians in remote districts, $65,000." There is a similar item for all the provinces where provision is made for the Indians. For Ontario and Quebec I find an item of $42,700 for "relief, medical attendance and medicines," and for Manitoba, Saskatchewan, Alberta and Northwest Territories an item of $140,000 for "supplies for destitute." Then there is an item of $11,000 for "relief in Nova Scotia, $10,000 for "relief" in New Brunswick, $13,000 for "relief and seed grain" in Prince Edward Island, and $22,000 for "relief to destitute" in British Columbia. Now I understand that in all the provinces except the Northwest Territories there is a regular organization to take care of these Indians. The remote districts would only be in the Northwest Territories, I presume, where the Indian population, according to the figures that have just been given, is only 3,309. Yet we find the sum of $65,000 allotted for relief to destitute Indians in remote districts. That relief work seems to be covered by item No. 263.

Mr. MEIGHEN: Not exactly. This item is intended to look after the Northwest Ter-

Fig 7

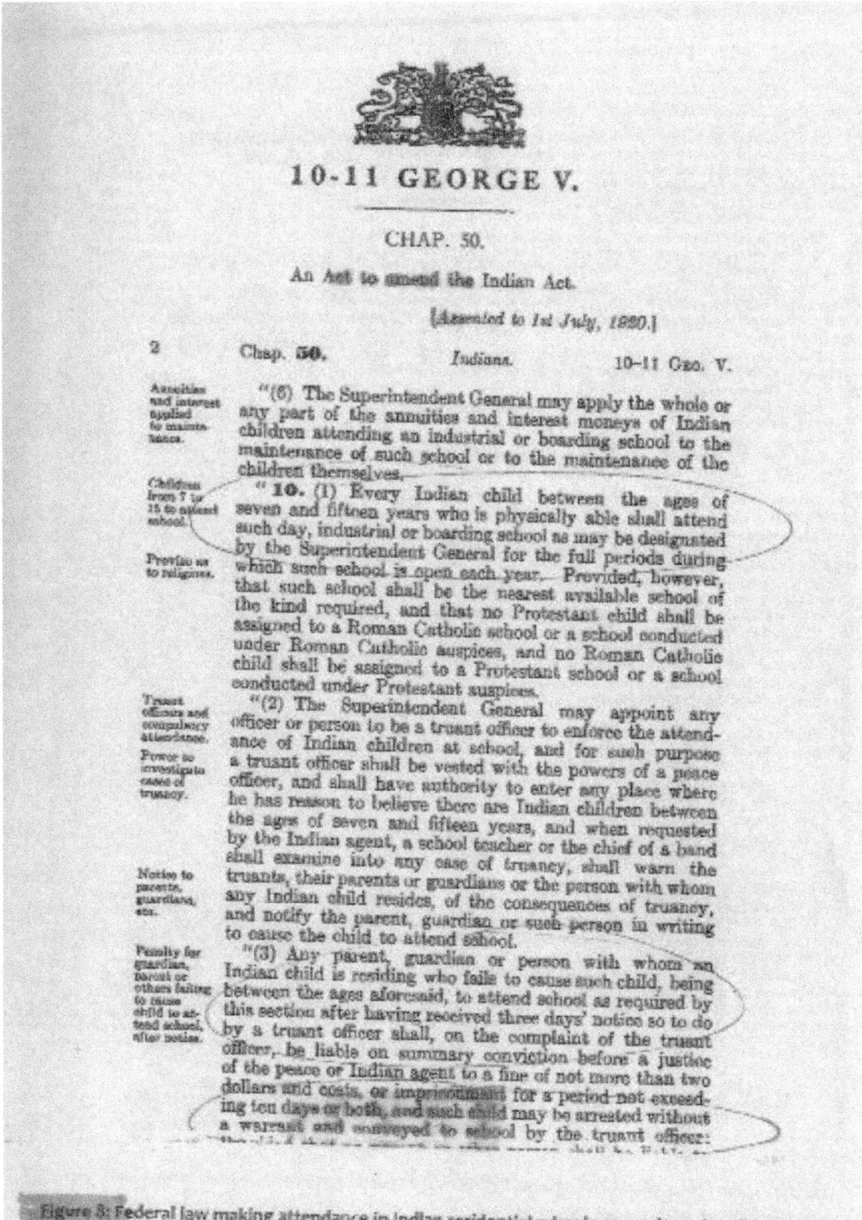

10-11 GEORGE V.

CHAP. 50.

An Act to amend the Indian Act.

[*Assented to 1st July, 1920.*]

2 Chap. 50. *Indians.* 10-11 Geo. V.

Annuities and interest applied to maintenance.

"(6) The Superintendent General may apply the whole or any part of the annuities and interest moneys of Indian children attending an industrial or boarding school to the maintenance of such school or to the maintenance of the children themselves.

Children from 7 to 15 to attend school.

"**10.** (1) Every Indian child between the ages of seven and fifteen years who is physically able shall attend such day, industrial or boarding school as may be designated by the Superintendent General for the full periods during which such school is open each year. Provided, however, that such school shall be the nearest available school of the kind required, and that no Protestant child shall be assigned to a Roman Catholic school or a school conducted under Roman Catholic auspices, and no Roman Catholic child shall be assigned to a Protestant school or a school conducted under Protestant auspices.

Proviso as to religion.

Truant officers and compulsory attendance.

Power to investigate cases of truancy.

"(2) The Superintendent General may appoint any officer or person to be a truant officer to enforce the attendance of Indian children at school, and for such purpose a truant officer shall be vested with the powers of a peace officer, and shall have authority to enter any place where he has reason to believe there are Indian children between the ages of seven and fifteen years, and when requested by the Indian agent, a school teacher or the chief of a band shall examine into any case of truancy, shall warn the truants, their parents or guardians or the person with whom any Indian child resides, of the consequences of truancy, and notify the parent, guardian or such person in writing to cause the child to attend school.

Notice to parents, guardians, etc.

Penalty for guardian, parent or others failing to cause child to attend school, after notice.

"(3) Any parent, guardian or person with whom an Indian child is residing who fails to cause such child, being between the ages aforesaid, to attend school as required by this section after having received three days' notice so to do by a truant officer shall, on the complaint of the truant officer, be liable on summary conviction before a justice of the peace or Indian agent to a fine of not more than two dollars and costs, or imprisonment for a period not exceeding ten days or both, and such child may be arrested without a warrant and conveyed to school by the truant officer:

Figure 8: Federal law making attendance in Indian residential schools compulsory for all native children seven years and older (1920)

Fig 8

A12 THE VANCOUVER SUN, WEDNESDAY, APRIL 26, 2000 — NATION

Native kids 'used for experiments'

A church magazine says federal health tests were conducted in B.C. and Ontario residential schools in the 1940s and '50s.

SOUTHAM NEWS, VANCOUVER SUN

OTTAWA — The federal government conducted health experiments on First Nations children in residential schools in the late 1940s and early '50s, a church magazine has reported. One of the four residential schools was located in Port Alberni.

Native children were deliberately denied basic dental treatment at the United Church-run Port Alberni school and scientists also "tinkered" with the children's diets at other schools, the *Anglican Journal* reports.

The government did not inform many of the parents of the research the government was conducting on their children.

In a letter on Oct. 3, 1949, Dr. H.K. Brown, chief of the dental health division of the federal health department, requested staff halt some dental treatments at the Port Alberni school, the *Journal* reports.

"No specialized, over-all type of dental service should be provided, such as the use of sodium fluoride, dental prophylaxis or even urea compounds," he wrote in his one-page letter. "In this study dental caries and gingivitis are both important factors in assessing nutritional status."

The *Anglican Journal* story quotes the doctor who headed the five-year research program, now a 90-year-old nursing home resident.

"It was not a deliberate attempt to leave children to develop caries [tooth decay] except for a limited time or place or purpose, and only then to study the effects of vitamin C or fluoride," said Dr. L.B. Pett, former chief of the nutritional division of the health department.

Pett acknowledged that "parental consent was not always obtained for those children involved in the study".

The revelation shocked George Erasmus, head of the Aboriginal Healing Foundation, which aids victims of residential school abuse. He told the *Journal* the experiments were unknown to him.

The objective of the research at Indian residential school children was "to evolve methods for improving health, not only of the school children but of the whole population," Pett said in the story.

In dietary experiments, federal health officials supplied flour with added vitamins in 1949-50. Then the vitamin supplements were halted so the results could be studied.

Fig 15

AT LARGE

Vancouver Sun, July 10, 1995

Minister who tried to bring natives into the fold fired by his church

STEPHEN HUME

PORT ALBERNI

Nuu-Chah-Nulth peoples have associated with the United Church since it dispatched fervent missionaries to snag souls in remote settlements a hundred years ago.

Yet Rev. Kevin McNamee-Annett, newly arrived in Port Alberni from an activist street ministry in Toronto, observed that almost no natives attended his new church.

"They never set foot in our church. I found that strange."

George Hamilton, a young native, returned from Vancouver's tough East Side streets to raise his kids. He says he felt the lash of Port Alberni's unspoken prejudice while he was growing up.

"As a kid, I don't remember one Indian face working in any of the stores in town. I still don't see any Indian faces working in any of the stores. But Kevin, Kevin didn't just have compassion for Indians. He had compassion for all the poor and weak."

Hamilton became one of McNamee-Annett's parishioners.

McNamee-Annett says he did set out to change things. He counselled abuse victims at the native friendship centre. He ran workshops. He started a food bank. Many of its users were native and he says he became close to them.

"In the poor part of the town and on the reserve some of the housing is the worst I've ever seen — and I've done urban ministries in Toronto, Vancouver and Winnipeg.

"I was involved in taking several slum landlords to arbitration and helping set up tenants' advocacy groups — that didn't sit well."

The new reverend began baptizing the poor, marrying the neglected, burying the dispossessed. His ministry took him into the wretched strip that natives call The Ghetto. It still seems invisible to Port Alberni's comfortable middle class.

"When nobody else spoke out," says Hamilton, "there was Kevin."

McNamee-Annett says he simply sought to ground lost souls in his church, welcoming them. Sunday attendance doubled. He told his flock to "learn to love them, up close. For love of the stranger is the only measure by which you and I will be judged."

Some of the congregation didn't like it. Loving strangers was okay in theory, it seems, but not in practice.

"To bring the natives into the pews was explosive," McNamee-Annett says. "The traditional congregation was fairly uptight."

McNamee-Annett says some families he encouraged to begin attending church services ran into a chilly climate. When he suggested at one board meeting that Ahousat elder Nelson Keitlah serve on a church committee the silence was "deafening."

One day a young woman from the poorest part of Port Alberni brought her little son to church. The baby cried, as babies do. This, McNamee-Annett says, did not bother him. But for some members of the congregation, it was a final, infuriating straw.

"Two women went to her and told her to get out. They said her baby was a little brat. 'Why did you bring him here, we don't want you.' They later came to me and threatened to leave if she stayed."

It was, he says, a dilemma to test his faith.

"It was 'suffer the little children to come unto me' versus good relations with the congregation."

He chose the young mother. One of his parishioners quit. On Jan. 5, he notified the church of his intention to resign effective June 30. Two weeks later, he says, he was summarily fired at the behest of six parishioners.

"The only reason church officials have given for this sudden, harsh action is that certain unidentified members of St. Andrew's had criticisms of my sermons and ministry."

At one point, the minister wrote a strong letter supporting the Ahousat band's objection to the church's sale, for substantial profit, of a property it had been more or less given by the native community for a school.

That, Keitlah believes, was the real source of his lack of support from the church hierarchy.

Church authorities decline to comment on the reasons for the firing. Authorities do confirm that it was not a disciplinary matter and that it had nothing to do with moral misconduct. They claim it was not connected to his ministry to poor natives.

"It's important to remember that there are good people here," says Keitlah. "People were kind to me."

But he admits he has stopped attending the church since McNamee-Annett was dismissed.

"My faith in God isn't shaken," Hamilton says, "but it is certainly shaken in the church. It was, 'Get them out of here! We don't want them here!' It was gross.

"I wouldn't paint the entire congregation with the same brush — there is a silent majority. It's an indictment of them that they were silent. I have no desire to attend that church."

"I think it's just atrocious what they did to him," says Jack McDonald of Port Alberni's Metis Association. "His actions spoke louder than words — so do theirs."

As for the jobless reverend?

McNamee-Annett says he will be preaching the gospel, church or no church.

"They've taken away my job but not my calling." □

Figure 18a: First media report of the firing without cause of Rev. Kevin Annett for bringing aboriginal people into his St. Andrew's United Church in Port Alberni, British Columbia (1995)

Fig 18a

THE GRANT REPORT (Centre for Philanthropy, Ottawa, …

…d Harvest Food Support Committee, Toronto, ON, *Poverty Relief* — $7,500

…d Mile Club of Toronto, Toronto, ON, *Social Services* — $7,500

…for the Visually Impaired, Etobicoke, ON, *Blind* — $6,255

…ed Way of Greater Toronto, Toronto, ON, *United Ways* — $6,000

SPORTS AND RECREATION

…ada Israel Athletics Fund, Concord, ON, *Sports* — $20,000

…Lynch Foundation; Walker

…information not available.

…M.Q.L. Foundation

1993 Grants

EDUCATION

McGill University, Montreal, PQ, *Universities* — $10,000

…M.S.I. Foundation; The

…information not available.

…MacDonald Foundation for Animal Welfare; The A.J.

…information not available.

…MacDonald Foundation; Richard and Mary

…information not available.

…Macdonald Stewart Foundation; The

…information not available.

…Machan Charitable Foundation …; The George

534 Mackenzie Memorial Foundation; The Ada

1993 Grants

SOCIAL SERVICES AND ISSUES

Canadian Wheelchair Sports Association, Vanier, ON, *Physically Disabled*	$50,000
Ontario Track Three Ski Association for the Disabled, Etobicoke, ON, *Disabled*	$20,000
CNIB, National Organization, Toronto, ON, *Blind*; Ontario Visually Impaired Golfers Association	$12,000

535 MacKinnon Foundation

1993 Grants

RELIGIOUS ORGANIZATIONS

Providence College & Seminary, Otterburne, MB, *Religious Education*	$8,800
Bethesda Church, Winnipeg, MB, *Churches*	$6,000

536 MacLennan Foundation; The Charles and Mary

Grant information not available.

537 MacMillan Family Fund; The

1993 Grants

EDUCATION

University of British Columbia, Vancouver, BC, *Universities*, Faculty of Forestry	$20,000
Western Canadian Universities, Marine Biological Society, Victoria, BC, *Universities*; Re: Bamfield Marine Station	$20,000

RELIGIOUS ORGANIZATIONS

First United Church, Port Alberni, BC, *United Churches and Organizations*	$8,000
Salvation Army, Public Relations	$5,000

* 1994-9…

Figure 18b: Payoff by MacMillan-Bloedel logging company to its business partner the United Church of Canada for receiving stolen land of the Ahousaht Indian nation (1995)

Fig 18b

To the editor:

As Kevin Annett's former wife, I feel compelled to respond to certain inaccuracies contained in Clodagh O'Connell's article *Maverick Minister* (Sept. 21 issue).

Contrary to what O'Connell wrote, at no time did I ever meet or talk with a lawyer or any other person representing the United Church regarding my divorce action. My lawyer did seek out and receive a report regarding Mr. Annett's suitability for ministry prepared by Comox-Nanaimo Presbytery, available to anyone interested in the matter.

ANNE MCNAMEE,
VANCOUVER

(The Vancouver Courier,
Sept. 28, 1997)

Figure 22: Admission by ex-wife of Kevin Annett that she colluded with the United Church of Canada to divorce Kevin and deprive him of his children (1997)

Fig 22

The New Internationalist, No. 309, Jan-Feb '99

Update

HUMAN RIGHTS

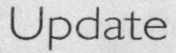

Disturbing revelations

Native Canadian nightmares see the light of day

UNITED Church minister Kevin Annett was puzzled to find no native members of St Andrew's Church when he arrived in Port Alberni, British Columbia, in 1992. Annett started asking local Native people why they had not attended church. Their answer – shocking stories of abuse and murder at the local church-run residential school.

As part of a government program of forced assimilation, Canadian Native children were taken from their homes and placed in residential schools which were operated by most of the major religions. It is estimated that up to 125,000 Native children passed through the system before it was closed down in the 1980s.

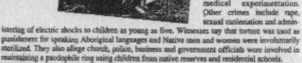

Waiting for justice to be done – Native Canadians on the streets of Vancouver.

KEVIN ANNETT

Now a tribunal has been established in British Columbia to investigate human-rights violations in the province's residential schools for Native children. So far over 30 people have given their eyewitness accounts.

The list of alleged offences is shocking. Eyewitness testimony and other evidence presented to the tribunal recount instances of murder by beating, poisoning, hanging, starvation, strangulation, being thrown from windows and medical experimentation. Other crimes include rape, sexual molestation and administering of electric shocks to children as young as five. Witnesses say that torture was used as punishment for speaking Aboriginal languages and Native men and women were involuntarily sterilized. They also allege church, police, business and government officials were involved in maintaining a paedophile ring using children from native reserves and residential schools.

Witnesses are regularly threatened and intimidated and Annett himself has received death threats. Annett was also fired from his job at the church. A recent suicide of abuse victim Darryl Watts, who had been badgered by Church lawyers, and the revelation that his parents never signed a release form to send him to the school led the United Church to issue 'apologies' to the survivors. At least 1,400 people are suing the Church and Government.

The tribunal eventually plans to publish its findings and present them to United Nations Human Rights Commissioner, Mary Robinson. Whatever happens at the UN, for the victims of these unimaginable horrors life can never be the same again.

Harriet Nahanee, 60, was the first witness to support the allegations about abuse and killings at the Alberni United Church school. She says she still has nightmares about the time she witnessed the death of a young girl who came from Nitinat Lake. 'I heard her crying. She was looking for her mother. I heard the school administrator yelling at the supervisor for letting the child run around on the stairwell. I heard him kick her and she fell down the stairs. I went to look – her eyes were open, she wasn't moving. I never saw her again.' ■

Alan Hughes

Figure 32: First international media coverage of Indian residential school crimes and Kevin Annett (*The New Internationalist*, January 1999)

Fig 32

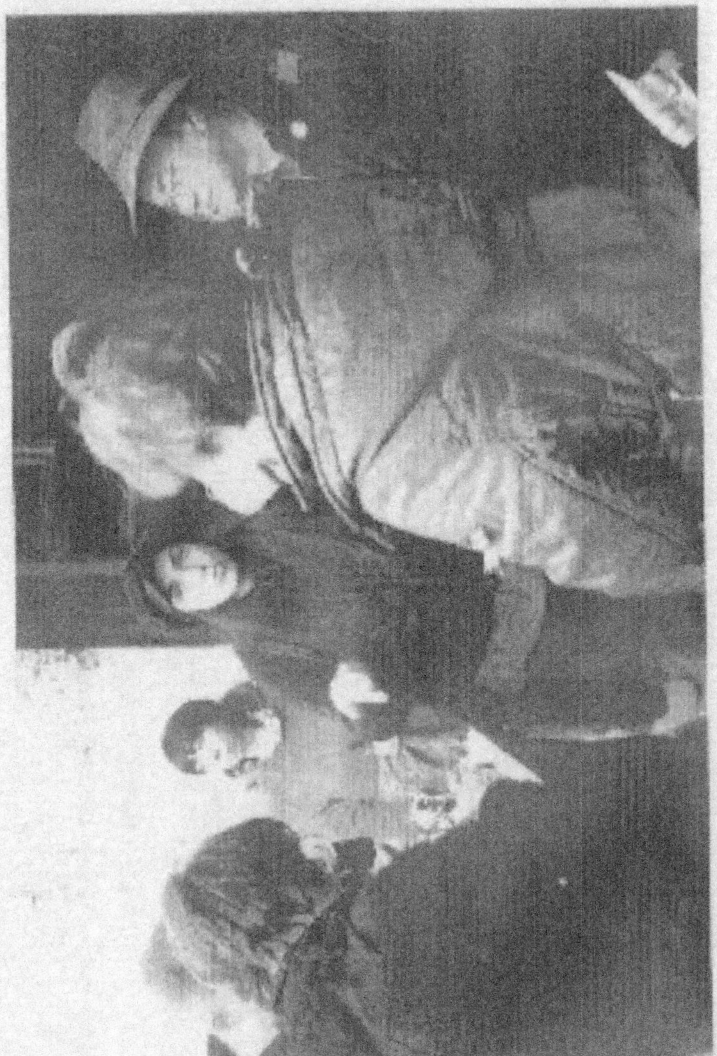

Italian State Police Disrupt planned vigil by Rev. Annett and others outside the Vatican, Rome, April 2010

Fig 47

BRITISH
COLUMBIA

June 15, 2010

Rev Kevin Annatt
260 Kennedy Street
Nanaimo, BC
V9R 2H8

Dear Rev Annatt:

Re: Coroner's Inquiry into the death of:
<u>DAWSON, Johnny Roy: BCCS #09-280-0149</u>

As per your request, I have enclosed a copy of the Coroner's Report and Toxicology Results. I trust these documents will provide you with the information you require.

If I can be of any assistance, please do not hesitate to contact this office.

Sincerely,

for Matt Brown
Coroner

Enclosure
jyd

Ministry of Public Safety and Solicitor General
BC Coroners Service
Vancouver Metro Region Coroners Office
Suite 800 - 4720 Kingsway
Burnaby, BC V5H 4N2
Phone: 604 660-7708
Facsimile: 604-660-5280
Web: www.pssg.gov.bc.ca/coroners

Figure 48: Coroner's report for Bingo Dawson, refuting cause of death claim of "alcohol poisoning"

Fig 48

THE INTERNATIONAL COMMON LAW COURT OF JUSTICE
CRIMINAL TRIAL DIVISION - BRUSSELS
FEBRUARY 25, 2013

VERDICT AND SENTENCE OF THE CITIZEN JURY

In the Matter of *The People v. the Government of Canada, the Crown of England, the Vatican, and the Roman Catholic, Anglican and United Church of Canada, and Joseph Ratzinger, Elizabeth Windsor, Stephen Harper and other persons*

We the Jury, consisting of fifty eight sworn men and women, having considered all of the evidence presented to us in this case, do hereby find all of the named defendants guilty as charged on both counts of the indictment, namely, of Crimes against Humanity and of planning and perpetrating a Criminal Conspiracy.

We the Jury therefore sentence all of the named defendants to a prison term of twenty five years without possibility of parole, and to a loss of all of their authority, assets and property.

We swear and acknowledge that this verdict and sentence was decided by we the Jury unanimously and without coercion or influence.

We further affirm that the following men and women are the defendants so tried and sentenced by us:

Jospeh Ratzinger, Bishop of Rome, aka "Pope Benedict"

Adolfo Nicholas Pachon, Superior General, Jesuit Order

Tarcisio Bertone, Vatican Secretary of State

Elizabeth Windsor, aka "Queen of England"

Stephen Harper, Prime Minister of Canada

Angelo Sodano, Vatican College of Cardinals

Angelo Bognasco, Vatican College of Cardinals

Pedro Lopez Quintana, Papal Nuncio to Canada

Rowan Williams, Archbishop of Canterbury

Figure 56: Guilty verdict issued by the International Common Law Court of Justice in Brussels against Joseph Ratzinger, Elizabeth Windsor and 28 other defendants (February 25, 2013)

Fig 57

THE SECRET SYSTEM

A secret system that protected clerical abusers had been in operation as far back as the seventeenth century, the founder of the Piarist Order Father Joseph Calasanz suppressed the sexual abuse of children by his priests so that it would not become public knowledge.

A member of a well known Vatican family Father Stefano Cherubini was one such priest who covered up his crimes so well he went on to become head of the order.

He was successful along with other priests in the abuse of children and it would take more than ten years before complaints would be taken seriously.

It was Pope Innocent X who took action and closed down the order temporarily, and a historian who showed that the secret system had a very modern ring to it including 'Promotion for Avoidance' in elevating the abuser away from the victim.

In 1962 the Holy Office went to great lengths to ensure total secrecy in what can only be described as horrendous crimes of abuse.

Up until the 1980s, Pope John Paul II and some of his cardinals and bishops chose to ignore many years of sexual abuse by priests.

Prior to 2002 Pope John Paul II defined the sexual abuse by priests as a 'Sin', then in April 2002 he finally acknowledged child abuse as a 'Crime'.

The Catholic Church have always looked after their own, offending clergy could not be brought before civil courts, unless permission was given.

In the early 1980s after years of deliberation the current Code of Cannon Law was published and amongst the changes was to drop the permission which is now a huge regret to the Catholic hierarchy.

This opened the doors for many more of the victims to come forward costing the church millions of dollars and continues to cost to this day.

It's extremely hard to take the church seriously when they themselves continue to break almost every rule in the book, while their own sins are coming back to haunt them it doesn't seem to faze them, still the abuse continues.

The Catholic Church and many other Institutions have faced significant scrutiny and criticism for many years over instances of abuse, one of the most prominent being the Boston archdiocese scandal in the 1980s.

In the early 2000s, a series of shocking allegations of sexual abuse by Catholic priests came to light in the Boston area. Several victims accused priests of sexually molesting them during their childhood and teenage years.

The allegations involved a significant number of priests, leading to a widespread scandal that rocked the community and the Church.

Some members of the clergy had engaged in a systematic cover-up and, in protecting accused priests by moving them to other dioceses without the knowledge of the community or law enforcement.

In the eyes of the victims and the community this was nothing more than protecting the abusers and the reputation of the church.

As public awareness of the Boston archdiocese scandal grew, legal actions were initiated against the church, these actions were to hold the church responsible for the atrocities committed by priests.

The church faced numerous lawsuits which resulted in financial settlements reaching millions of dollars, including highlighting the magnitude and scale of the abuse.

Boston was not an isolated case, it soon became apparent that this was a worldwide issue and, prompted many other victims to come forward.

In 2019 Chile removed its statute of limitations on child sex abuse, Chilean President Sebastian Pinera signed into law a bill to remove the statute of limitations on sex crimes involving children amid a sex abuse crisis that rocked the country's Catholic Church which claimed more than 200 victims.

The law, which first proposed in 2010, ends impunity in cases that would have previously had a statute of limitations that varied between five and ten years, depending on the nature of the crime.

In 2018, a church-commissioned report concluded that at least 3,677 people were abused by the clergy in Germany between 1946 and 2014 (*These figures are most likely to be more as many will not have talked about their abuse*).

More than half of the victims were aged 13 or younger, and nearly a third served as alter boys.

An internal investigation published identified 728 alleged sexual abusers amongst the Spanish clergy and 927 victims since in the 1940s, that followed a report in EI Pais Newspaper that identified more than 1,200 alleged cases.

On 5 October 2021, the Independent Commission on Sexual Abuse in the French Catholic Church published a report, it’s revelations were horrifying.

From 1950 to 2020, no less than 330,000 minors were victims of sexual abuse by clerics or laypersons within the church.

According to the Bishop Accountability it has identified 93 priests and brothers in the Republic of Ireland and Northern Ireland who have been convicted of sexually abusing children or whose alleged abuses have been amply documented in the Ferns, Ryan, Murphy and Cloyne reports. (*Worth a read*).

They have their own list of accused priests which I myself have read through and was astonished at the figures and this is just a few…

Fr Andrew Allen. Armagh

On missionary duty in Trinidad and Tobago. Plead guilty to four sample charges of indecent assault on two brothers in 1981-1985. Given a two-year suspended sentence and ordered to pay £150,000 compensation. The brothers had been abused by Allen during his visits back to Ireland. He had been jailed for a year in Drogheda in 1993 for sexually assaulting an altar boy in 1991-1992.

Br Stephen Allen. Dublin

Sentenced to one year in prison in March 2009 for sexually abusing four boys in 1961-1964 at an industrial school.

Fr Ronald Bennett. Dublin

Bursar, spiritual director, and sports master at Gormanston College in Co. Meath, a secondary boarding school run by the Franciscans. Pleaded guilty of sexual abuse and was jailed in 2007. Sexually abused at least 6 boys.

Fr John (Dominic Savio) "Domo" Boland

Boland was convicted in 2001, of 9 counts of indecent assault of a boy age 11 in 1977-1979. The conviction and one-year suspended sentence were apparently not reported by the Capuchins, the Dublin archdiocese, or the press. So the 2009 Murphy report was the first public information about serial offender Boland, although he first molested a boy in 1946, when Boland was age 16. In the 8 years between his conviction and Murphy, Boland visited at least one family 'On a regular basis'.

The Murphy report described 6 complaints of abuse by Boland and 2 'suspicions/concerns', altogether involving 9 victims whose names were known to the Commission - 8 boys and 1 girl. But 2 victims - a girl at a school retreat and a boy in a boy's club - reported that there were other victims. In addition, the matron of a hospital and a mother visiting a hospital both expressed concern about Boland's behavior with children. According to the Murphy report, a 'UK therapeutic facility' said in 1996 that Boland admitted about 100 offenses against 20 children.

The Murphy report also described Boland's methods as he detailed them to the UK facility. He used 'Holy medals and pictures' (32.17) to engage children, befriended their parents, separated the child, and introduced and normalised sexual touching. He had a well-developed belief system which supported and legitimised his sexual interest in children.

An account after the Murphy report describes Boland's saintly reputation, devotion to the Virgin Mary, Christ-like beard, use of relics, and power to heal the sick. 'Mothers loved him' and raised money in bake sales and the like to buy him a car despite his vow of poverty. 'Parents considered him both harmless and trustworthy.' He organized a boys soccer team in Dublin's Northside inner city that traveled all over the country and abroad. Boland's left arm was paralysed in a birth injury, a 'distinguishing physical characteristic' cited in the Murphy report, which he considered a blessing. 'Out of devotion to his Italian boy-hero saint, [he] had taken the adolescent's name, Dominic Savio, as his own.' The Murphy report states that he claimed he'd been 'frequently abused at age 8'.

Boland's charisma was apparently at work in his suspended sentence, the failure to report his conviction, and the continued free movement afforded him by that silence. Much remains unknown about his whereabouts (e.g., his fill-in work at parishes), the lack of coordination between the Capuchins and the dioceses, the documents lost from the files, etc. The Murphy report discusses 2 Boland child victims who went on to join religious orders (The Capuchins and another unnamed religious institute). The persuasiveness of Boland's religious example and his extensive abusive behavior merit more attention.

The list goes on and on.

While now we are seeing SOME changes within the church in how it deals with sexual abuse it doesn't mean that the secret system has been eradicated.

The Vatican's Secret Archives were first collected and stored in some systematic order in Rome's Castel San't Angelo (Hadrian's Tomb), in 1611-1614 they were moved to the Vatican.

We are led to believe that there are many secrets held in the Vatican with sexual abuses being one of its biggest secrets.

The atrocities of the clergy are like water off a ducks back when it comes to the church, lessons have not been learned, because they continue to ignore the one factor in all abuses caused by clergy, that being, the victims mental wellness.

The church doesn't seem to understand or acknowledge the profound impact on the abuse victims or their families.

Instead of holding the perpetrators to account and helping the victims to recover from such horrendous acts of abuse, they ship the abuser off to another diocese.

What they fail to realise (*Or perhaps they do*)? That the abuser is free to carry out such acts in the new diocese leaving that congregation unaware that they have a sexual predator on their watch.

In the eyes of a child, a priest is someone they should trust because they represent God, unfortunately the priest use their position of power and trust to scare children into thinking its what they are meant to do.

The church wonder why the congregation is whittling away, let's be honest, would you send your child to church unaccompanied? I wouldn't because they have lost my and many others trust.

THE GAUTHE CASE

It was while reading and researching the Gauthe case of 1985/86 in which 1,200 paedophile priests were exposed that I came across an article in The New York Times Archives.

Note about Archives:

This is a digitised version from The Times's print archives, before the start of online publication in 1996. To preserve these articles as they originally appeared, The Times do not alter, edit or update them.

Occasionally the digitisation process introduces transcription errors or other problems; we are not continuing to work or improve these archived versions.

The admission by a Roman Catholic priest that he sexually abused 37 children entrusted to his care has aroused a deep sense of betrayal and shame in this small rural community in southwestern Louisiana.

Alter boys and members of the parish Boy Scout troop were among those molested by the Rev. Gilbert Gauthe, 40 years old, according to felony charges of sexual abuse lodged against him by the local authorities.

Father Gauthe, who has been suspended by his Bishop and is currently confined to a private psychiatric hospital in Connecticut, has pleaded not guilty by reason of insanity to 34 counts of molestation.

If convicted, he could face life imprisonment and hard labour.

Assuming the case reaches trial stage - no date has yet Been set, it may be the first time that a priest has faced such charges in an

American court of law, according to the National Catholic Reporter, which has carried a number of articles on the case.

Meanwhile, aggrieved parents are suing the local diocese, seeking compensation and treatment for their abused children.

So far the diocese and its insurance companies have paid $4.2 million to the families of nine children. But more than a dozen additional civil suits have been filed as more families overcome their hesitance to seek redress from a church that has been a bedrock of their lives.

Lawyers for the parents now say that, over several years, as many as 70 children were assaulted by Father Gauthe in hundreds of acts of sodomy, rape and photographing of sexual acts.

Anguish and seething anger have also been directed at the church after it was learned that Father Gauthe had been reassigned to St. John's, the parish church of Henry, after suspicions were raised about his behaviour with young boys at two parishes he served previously.

The Rt. Rev. Gerard Frey, Bishop of the Lafayette Diocese, acknowledged in a legal deposition taken in connection with the civil suit that he confronted the priest in 1974.

The priest, according to the Bishop, admitted he was guilty of "Imprudent Touches" with a young man and vowed it was an isolated case that would not recur.

The following year the Bishop appointed Father Gauthe chaplain of the diocese Boy Scouts.

In 1977, the year before he was moved to Henry, similar complaints were made by parents to the priest's superiors, and Father Gauthe was directed to seek psychiatric treatment.

A Louisiana judge had ordered the principals in the suits not to comment, and the diocesan office of Lafayette said it had been asked by the insurance companies to remain silent.

But the case had stirred national currents of concern within the church.

A reminder in New Jersey.

"We don't want to give the impression that it's a rampant problem for the church, because it is not." Said the Rev. Kenneth Doyle, a spokesperson for the United States Catholic Conference in Washington. *"But even one case is too many"*

Last month in New Jersey Catholic Conference issued guidelines to parochial school principles and teachers, reminding them of the requirement of complying with the state's child abuse reporting law, which charges all citizens with the responsibility of reporting acts of child abuse to the authorities.

The guidelines also instructed that similar reports be made to school superintendents or the diocese office if church "employees, priests, nuns and lay teachers" were involved, according to William Nolan, Executive director of the state conference.

It is feared by some in the church that publicity over the Louisiana case and the resultant suits may encourage families of child abuse victims everywhere to seek damages.

Just last week another priest in Louisiana who runs a home for boys returned to Florida to face a felony charge that he sexually assaulted a 10-year old Tampa boy last year.

"The tragedy and Scandal," The National Catholic Reporter said in editorial last week on the Louisiana case, "Is not only with the actions of the individual priests - these are serious enough - but with the church structures in which Bishops, Chanceries and Seminaries fail to respond to complaints, or even engage in cover-ups."

Periodic Review Suggested.

Some of the victims were as young as 7 years old, according to parents and investigators.

A lawyer involved in the case, who asked not to be identified, said he hoped the revelations would encourage the church to reconsider periodically the competency of its priests.

"If school boards can recertify teachers after 15 years, why can't the church review the competency of its priests?" Asked the lawyer.

F. Ray Mouton Jr. of Lafayette, the lawyer hired by the church to represent the priest at the upcoming trial, said his client was determined not to do anything that might further damage the children.

"He's going to admit it all," Mr Mouton said. " We will prove that he did those things. To do otherwise would force all these kids to come into the courtroom and testify.

Henry, situated on the edge of the freshwater marshes and bayous not far from the Gulf of Mexico, is a sparsely settled, French-speaking community connected by road and ferry to the few hundred residents in the hamlet of Esther, who were also served by Father Gauthe.

The disclosures have been devastating for two communities made of hard-working farmers and oilfield workers.

Change the attitude.

Reactions to the scandal have been deeply divided, Glenn and Faye Gastal, who owned the local feed store, were forced out of business after they were among the parents to make public the sexual abuse of their son, now 10.

Resentment ran high, the Gastal's said, among those who felt it wrong to attack the church in public.

"Neighbour have been set against neighbour" said one man close to the situation who asked not to be identified.

Nearly everyone in this corner of Vermillion Parish, speaking out in public on the emotionally charged case is regarded as foolhardy.

"At first everyone wanted to circle the wagons and protect the church," he observed. "Then they were afraid the civil suits would be taking money out of their own pockets because they are the ones who support the diocese.

But the mood has changed, now they want to know what the church has done to make sure this kind of crime never happens again.

Inevitably, said another resident, "A big guessing game developed over which kids were involved with the priest," and a sense of guilt drove the children to protect their secret with ever-growing shame.

There is now growing concern that the abused children will face psychological problems.

"I think these children are like Humpty-Dumpty they have been broken and to some extent they may not be put back together again," said Raul R. Bencomo, one of the lawyers who won the $4.2 million settlement fro the church.

"Children who have been abused, particularly by a figure of authority, someone they called Father, go through several phases of guilt. A lot of the kids have very deep-rooted guilt feelings."

One of the abused boys had been sent to a hospital in Texas for treatment of emotional disturbance that his parents say was produced by the trauma of his relations with the priest.

On further research.

A life sentence: An Ohio priest who coerced three boys into engaging in sexual acts as children and abused their addictions to opioids as teenagers and adults, paying them money that funded their drug habits in exchange for sex, was sentenced to life in prison.

Filing for bankruptcy: The archdiocese of Baltimore, the oldest in the United States, filed for bankruptcy days before the start of a new state law removing the statute of limitations on lawsuits from abused victims. (*How convenient*).

U.S. Investigations: About 20 state attorneys general, including those in Illinois and Maryland, have mounted investigations that have cataloged decades of abuse.

The more I research the more I'm finding that the church and often the state are indeed being successfully sued and being held to account for the decades of abuse on children.

That said, its by far not enough and we have a long way to go in bringing the perpetrators to face the consequences of their actions.

I am angry as are many others that, although SOME of the clergy are being given a prison sentence, the church are not showing any remorse for the suffering inflicted not only on the child, but their families when it all comes out in the wash.

My question has always been, why are they allowing most priests to continue to abuse by moving them to other dioceses, yet, others are being jailed?

Is it because they have to be seen to be punishing SOME of the clergy so that it looks better on them, do they feel the victims and survivors of such abuses will be satisfied by thinking "okay, so the church are doing something about it?"

The only way to STOP these abuses is to first agree to them being prosecuted and then strip them of their ordination, period!

The congregation of the Catholic Church and some others are slowly falling away, not from their faith, but from the church itself, and the church are never going to agree to prosecution of all who commit these crimes.

Why? Because they stand to lose billions, they have and are already losing millions in compensation payments and stand to lose so much more.

EMOTIONAL RETURN

On 13 Sept, 2022 Myself, my husband, and many others gathered for a day of remembrance for the mother and baby home in Sean Ross Abbey, Tipperary.

Accompanied by survivors including Patrick McDermott who now resides in Santa Fe, New Mexico.

It was a very sad, yet poignant day which included a tour of Corville House, I had previously took part in the first visit to the house back in 2019, so I kind of knew what to expect.

It was no different to my first visit with that familiar dark, cold feeling, a feeling of pain, heartbreak and despair.

Patrick, now a good friend of myself and my husband Jerry has kindly allowed me to include some of his story that he read on the day of remembrance.

I was born in Sean ross Abbey in 1953, and sent to the U.S for adoption in 1957.

Sister Hildegarde was the Mother Superior during those years and handled the correspondence with my adoptive family.

In the months before my departure for the U.S, she wrote a letter to my adoptive parents that offered the following observations of what to expect from me.

"You are getting a very nice little boy and I trust you will like him, I don't think you will have any trouble with him but there is just one thing I would like to mention, and it is this - speak slowly to him for a while, you see, you do speak strangely when compared with our way of speaking, with you it is all rush, with us it is any old time will do" so remember that, it will help a lot.

Pat does not have a lot of unnecessary talk like a number of children, but he thinks a lot and can remember when many would forget.

We will get him out in company with some of his companions, in this way they will be company for each other, and the one guardian will do for all and you will have only part guardian fare to pay."

That perceptiveness Sister Hildegarde speaks of meant that at nearly 4 years of age she judged me as capable of a certain degree of understanding and remembering.

Unfortunately, no explanation was provided of what was to be a seismic shift in my life.

I have no memories of my childhood in Ireland, my mother Maire McDermott was at Sean Ross for all these years, but I don't remember her.

That's because others and children were forbidden from developing attachments, although allowed to see their children one hour a day, it is hard to know what they told their children.

Even memories of other children are lost to me. ironically, the only oral history of my nearly four years in Ireland is contained in that brief letter from Sister Hildegarde.

I flew to the U.S with 3 other children and a guardian. We were met at the airport by our adopted families.

My first vague memories are of enthusiastic strangers, with eager good intentions, but little understanding of what I was experiencing.

They called me their child and identified themselves as my parents, it was just too much to process and I remember a feeling of deep dread.

I was reportedly not willing to enter my parents home, and my adoptive father had to walk me up and down the street until my hunger made a promise of food irresistible.

With no family or friends to explain what had transpired, or what the future would bring this must have been a lonely experience.

I recall an awareness that it was best not to resist these new circumstances as my fate was obviously completely in the hands of strangers.

There were some signs of the trauma I was undergoing, I slept under the bed in my new Chicago home for most of the first year in the U.S.

I had nightmares for many years and built a deep distrust of strangers and social uncertainties.

I struggled with learning and developed a stutter in early grade school, my Irish accent must have set me apart and this may have had a role in my speech impediment.

Neighbours in these early years also frequently expressed concerns that I would always mention going home to Ireland as I played with their children!

I remember a stern lecture from my adoptive parents to forget any such nonsense. That door was firmly closed behind me.

I do remember my adoptive family as caring people who provided a stable upbringing, they were open about details of my adoption and both were of Irish American descent.

I will always be appreciative of their kindness, years later, I came to realise it was their church that recruited them for this adoption.

Prior to my arrival, they had adopted an infant through Catholic Charities, so there was some expectation that another child would balance things out.

Unfortunately for them I wasn't, and in fact as was their other adopted son. My American brother had been adopted shortly after his birth, instead I was already a distinct person and raised in a foreign country.

They were also misled by carefully shaped stories of the New World bailing out the Old World; of mothers dying in childbirth and homeless waifs in need of shelter.

With this narrative in their minds, it was no wonder they were mystified by my distance and defensiveness. The carefully crafted orphan story was fiction.

My parents felt misled when the story of places like Sean Ross emerged in the late 1970s.

They were candid with me then, emphasising that they would never have got involved if they understood the circumstances of my separation from my mother.

In hindsight, I believe it was especially cruel to involve such unsuspecting people in this adoption subterfuge. As devout Catholics, it must have felt like a betrayal.

I found my mother Maire in the 90s and corresponded with her, though ultimately she discouraged a visit to Ireland. After her death I visited Drumshambo, where she grew up and spent the last years of her life.

I met neighbours who had known my family, and the McDermotts never revealed my existence to friends or even other family members.

I was blessed to find the rest of my Irish birth family in Ireland, and the U.S, and they have welcomed me with open hearts.

I also have drawn a great deal of strength from peer support systems with other survivors, finally, I have a long term, unfailing partner in my spouse.

She has encouraged me and supported me emotionally throughout this long quest for rediscovery of my heritage.

She asked me to tell you that with 8% Irish DNA and 1% welsh, she too has roots in this part off the world.

Martin Luther King, a leader in the U.S civil Rights Movement, made a historic speech in which he observed that the arc of the moral universe is long but bends in the direction of justice.

The Bible also assures us that ultimately all secrets are revealed.

Today's gathering is a sign that this is indeed true, what the struggle is now, is that justice can be achieved.

In our history as human beings, it is often the weakest members of society, the woman and the children that bear the worst brunt of atrocities.

It should not be forgotten that the men who fathered and abandoned us were never held accountable for their absence and lack of protection for the child they helped create.

How can Ireland and the Catholic Church now make proper reparations? The scars and trauma of the past still live today in the survivors.

Worst yet, there are many that lay in mass graves whose existence has been erased from human memory.

My involvement in this project is due to my conviction that as a survivor, I have an obligation to ensure that those who lost their lives are never forgotten.

While atonement for sins is ultimately decided by God, we have an obligation as human beings to try to set things right and comfort the afflicted.

While some may argue that what was done to us was with the best intentions, the ultimate outcome was great suffering as woman were forcibly parted from their children.

We have no idea whether subsequent adoptions turned out well or the ultimate fate of these children.

I want to thank all of you for listening to my story. There's now legislation designed to help all of us in our quests for answers, I pray this legislation will help all of us in healing, as well as a firm commitment to preventing future abuse of woman, children and those most vulnerable in our world.

Patrick McDermott

Photo Credit: OFFLAY EXPRESS

Pictured outside Corville House where Patrick was born in 1953 before being sent for adoption to Chicago, Patrick was accompanied by his wife Dr. Bianca McDermott.

Patrick was welcomed home by Sinn Fein leader Mary Lou McDonald, followed by founder of 'We Are Still Here' Teresa Collins and TD Martin Browne at the Angel's Plot.

Patrick & his wife Dr. Bianca McDermott

Patrick, Bianca with Sinn Fein's Mary Lou McDonald

Teresa Collins founder of We Are Still Here with Mary Lou McDonald and TD Martin Browne

Addressing the gathering Mary Lou McDonald spoke with heartfelt emotion saying; “I am very taken and moved by Patrick’s story and by Bianca for your strength, your integrity and also your compassion.

“For me that has been the standout mark of all those I have met that were born here, or adopted from here, or who were trafficked from institutions like this.

“Because despite the fear and the horror and the cruelty of Mother and Baby Homes, the real legacy is the enduring humanity and the profound dignity of the survivors and it is their bravery that continues to expose the truth so that Ireland can confront and learn from the appalling way the State treated woman and children not too long ago.”

On the steps of Corville House Mary Lou said; “ It is their courage that allows us to stand here today to not only commemorate, but to also say confidently that we will get to the full point of the truth, justice and healing.

“These places were not homes, home is a place where you are respected and loved, protected, safe and nurtured.

Our job now is to ensure survivors and their families feel love and dignity and protection of a real home, and Patrick, you are home.”

NOBODY'S CHILD

In 2018 Nuns were among twelve people charged by detectives investigating alleged child abuse at a Catholic children's home in Lanarkshire, Scotland.

Allegations of systematic physical and sexual abuse of children over a period of years at Smyllum Park Orphanage.

I first heard of this Orphanage in 2017 after my first visit to Sean Ross abbey in Tipperary (An event I now attend every year) being the commemorations of the mother and baby home.

I was shocked to find that the Orphanage was only seven miles from my own home, I knew then that I had to find out more and made it my mission to do just that.

On Saturday 5, August 2023 I attended their memorial service for the 400 children from Smyllum buried in a mass grave at St Mary's Cemetery in Lanark.

It was a very sad yet poignant day and it had a good turn out, it wasn't just in memory of the children, a stone was laid in memory of Mr Frank Doherty 1944-2017 Honorary President of INCAS.

The stone for the children reads as follows;

In Memory of

The Deceased Children of Smyllum

Who Died Between 1864-1981

Their life so short, no world to roam,

Taken so young, they never went home,

So spare a thought for them as you pass this way,

A prayer, if you remember, day by day,

Yes, lives so short, bereft of love,
But found in the arms of the Lord God above.

Jesus said:-

"Suffer little children and forbid them not to come unto me, for of such is the kingdom of heaven.

Dedicated to the children of Smyllum, the sisters of charity and the abuse survivors.

Sunday Post Article Sept 10, 2017

Up to 400 children who died at an orphanage run by nuns were buried in an unmarked grave, we can reveal today.

Hundreds of babies, toddlers and teenagers from the Smyllum Park Orphanage home were laid to rest at a nearby cemetery.

Politicians, former residents and relatives of the children yesterday called for an immediate inquiry.

One relative said; *"It's horrific and heartbreaking, why have we been forced to wait so long for the truth?"*

This is indeed the dark side of the white collar and I have heard a number of stories from survivors.

I have spoke to several survivors and every one of them said the nuns and the priest were bastards.

Children were often beaten, punished for little to nothing and locked in cupboards, some were even made to eat their vomit.

One woman said; *"We would have carbolic soap shoved in our mouth"*. The children were often dragged by the hair if they were too ill to do chores.

Priests were known to take youngsters into a room and have their wicked way with them, this didn't happen only in Smyllum, this went on with girls and boys in various orphanages and boys school's.

The worst part was the passing of these children from one priest to another, if the priest was caught by a nun performing these sexual abuses, it was the child who was punished.

Children have accidents and it was no different in these homes, in fact, the only difference being that they were often made to sleep in their soiled beds sometimes for days, as well as being punished.

One gentleman I had correspondence with told me of his time there, for privacy reasons I cannot print the mans name but I can write about some of what we discussed.

This man at the time was in his 70s and trust me when I tell you, I had to bite the side of my mouth to stop myself crying as he cried while telling me parts of his story.

He was incarcerated into a particular orphanage around the age of six, he was badly beaten by nuns and sodomised by the priest on a regular basis.

He saw some of the most unthinkable of atrocities on other children, one of whom suddenly disappeared after a serious beating by a nun.

There is speculation that the boy may have been murdered, he took a severe beating for something he took the blame for to save another child.

The next day children had asked where this boy was to be told, he had gone home to his parents, that didn't wash with the other children, when they last saw him he was took to bed in the evening, when they got up in the morning he was gone.

For a lot of children in these orphanages run by the Catholic Church there was an ongoing lie that came from the nuns, the children were often told that their parents were either dead or didn't want the child.

I can only imagine what that would have been like for those children, it was bad enough feeling rejected living in these homes, nobody's arms to hug them and make them feel safe.

Many of the children who were put into these orphanages were not by any means orphans, many came from very poor families who's parents thought they would be looked after, fed and clothed in the homes.

The Daughters of Charity of St Vincent de Paul ran Smyllum Orphanage from 1864 until it's closing in 1981.

I often wonder just how many children suffered such atrocities in their care during those years.

One man described to the BBC how a nun kicked his face and body, he pleaded with her to stop.

The last update was posted by Police Scotland Lanarkshire on their Facebook page was as follow…

Three woman were yesterday, Wednesday, 13 December 2023, found guilty of cruel and unnatural treatment of children who were under their care at the former orphanage, Smyllum Park, in Lanark.

At Airdrie Sheriff Court, following a trial which lasted six weeks, Sister Sarah McDermott, 79 carer Margaret Hughes, 76 and Sister Eileen Igoe, 79 were found guilty of the charges relating to children in their care.

The incidents happened at the orphanage between 1969 and 1981 while children were in the care of the Daughters of Charity of St Vincent de Paul. (The victims included boys and girls).

Detective Inspector Jim McLauchlan said: "This has been a complex case and I would like to commend the courage of the survivors who have had to recall and revisit traumatic periods of their lives during the trial."

Orphaned children were placed in the care of those running Smyllum House which was supposed to be a place of safety.

The punishments and cruelty they suffered at such a young age was incomprehensible and has affected many of the survivors throughout their lives.

Investigating events from decades ago presents challenges and it can sometimes only be in hindsight that people recognise what happened to them was abuse.

Police Scotland have highly trained, specialist officers, across the country who can investigate such offences and, working with partners, ensure perpetrators are brought to justice.

The police response to the reports of childhood abuse has evolved significantly over the years and we would like to reassure survivors that we are committed to investigating all reports regardless of when it happened, where it took place or who was involved.

We will listen, we will investigate and we will take prompt action to ensure that no-one else is at risk of harm.

We would ask anyone wishing to report abuse to contact us on 101.

McDermott, Hughes, and Igoe are due to be sentenced at a later date.

Entrance to St Mary's Cemetery

Group gathering

God bless the little children

In Memory of Frank Docherty

ACKNOWLEDGEMENTS

I would like to thank Mary Lawlor from Tullamore who first brought to my attention the story behind the mother and baby homes, without that I would never have known exactly what took place in these institutions.

Also, Teresa Collins and Michael Donovan from Tipperary, who have worked tirelessly for the survivors of the mother and baby homes, and for their continued friendship to both myself and Jerry.

To Patrick McDermott for allowing me to include his speech in this book along with photography. And to those who were happy for me to add a small contribution on their stories.

Lastly**, Kevin D. Annett** who not only fathered and led the movements from the beginning at enormous personal risk and sacrifice but who also brought to light 'Murder by Decree' and allowed material from his book to be used in quotations for the purpose of educating those who are unaware.

Belinda Conniss Aka A.J McGinty

ABOUT THE AUTHOR

Since childhood Belinda's *(Also known as A.J McGinty)* passion was to one day write at least one book, fast forward to 2015, when she published her first book 'Sad, Lonely & a Long Way From Home'.

She has since gone on to publish several more in various Genre's including fiction, non-fiction and poetry.

Her writing has taken her on a journey which has allowed her to become an advocate and supporter of the survivors of Religiously Run Institutions, which in turn has led her on the path of investigative journalism.

Belinda has also gone on to study forensic psychology, and currently studying investigating psychology and human rights in law.

Belinda is now in the process of writing a heptalogy series of books with the first 'House of Annie Linn Bird' due for publication in 2024, under the name A.J McGinty.

OTHER BOOKS BY THIS AUTHOR

Under the pseudonym name Belinda Conniss:

BEHIND CLOSED DOORS (Non-Fiction)
THE EMPTY SWING (Fiction)
TEARS ON MY PILLOW (Poetry)
WHERE WATER FLOWS AND GRASS GROWS (Poetry)
SECRETS AND LIES (Autobiography Pt.2)
SAD, LONELY & A LONG WAY FROM HOME (Auto' Pt.1)

Under: A.J McGinty

CHASING HORIZONS (Poetry)
ROSIE CHASING RAINBOWS (Children's Book)

COMING SOON!

HOUSE OF ANNIE LINN BIRD (Fiction)
(First in a heptalogy series)
SIMPLE COOKING (Cookbook)
(My journey with food after my diagnosis)
RAT INFESTED BRITAIN (Non-Fiction)
THE UNHEARD SCREAMS OF THE ASYLUM (Non-Fiction)

Printed in Great Britain
by Amazon

35855364R00056